STAND TALL, DREAM BIG, THINK LARGE, I DARE YOU!

THINK LARGE INTERNATIONAL INC.
P.O. BOX 201852
SHAKER HEIGHTS, OH 44120

STAND TALL, DREAM BIG, THINK LARGE, I DARE YOU!

We Can All Be CHAMPIONS

Byron Jackson

THINK LARGE INTERNATIONAL
SHAKER HEIGHTS, OHIO

Copyright © 2008 by Byron Jackson.

ISBN: Softcover   978-1-4257-8703-5

All rights reserved,

Including the right of reproduction in whole or in part in any form. No part of this publication may be reproduced, stored in a retrieval system, transmitted in any form, or by any means without prior written permission of the author.

Jackson, Byron:
STAND TALL, DREAM BIG, THINK LARGE I DARE YOU!

Edited by: Constance L. Motley, and Zoretta L. Peterson.

Cover photo taken by Ashley J. Goodman.

Neither the author nor publisher assumes any responsibility for the use or misuse of information and sources contained in this book.

This book was printed in the United States of America.

To order additional copies of this book, contact:
THINK LARGE INTERNATIONAL INC.
P.O. BOX 201852
SHAKER HEIGHTS, OHIO 44120
770-714-1157:PH

Contents

Chapter 1 Goals 19
   The significance of Goal setting

Chapter 2 Confidence 28
   Strengthen your state of mind

Chapter 3 Attitude...33
   Thinking your way into success

Chapter 4 Take Action 40
   Acting on your goals, and proving yourself worthy for success

Chapter 5 Comfort Zone 44
   Never stop striving for excellence

Bonus Chapter for Parents and Guardians Only:
   Full Proof Program 48
   Ensuring your child's success

Author's Accomplishments 53

DEDICATION

This book is dedicated to the youths of America who want to become one of the leaders of tomorrow, and live the American Dream.

And to my mom and dad, Thank-You for your continuous motivation and support; for you are truly the foundation of my strength.

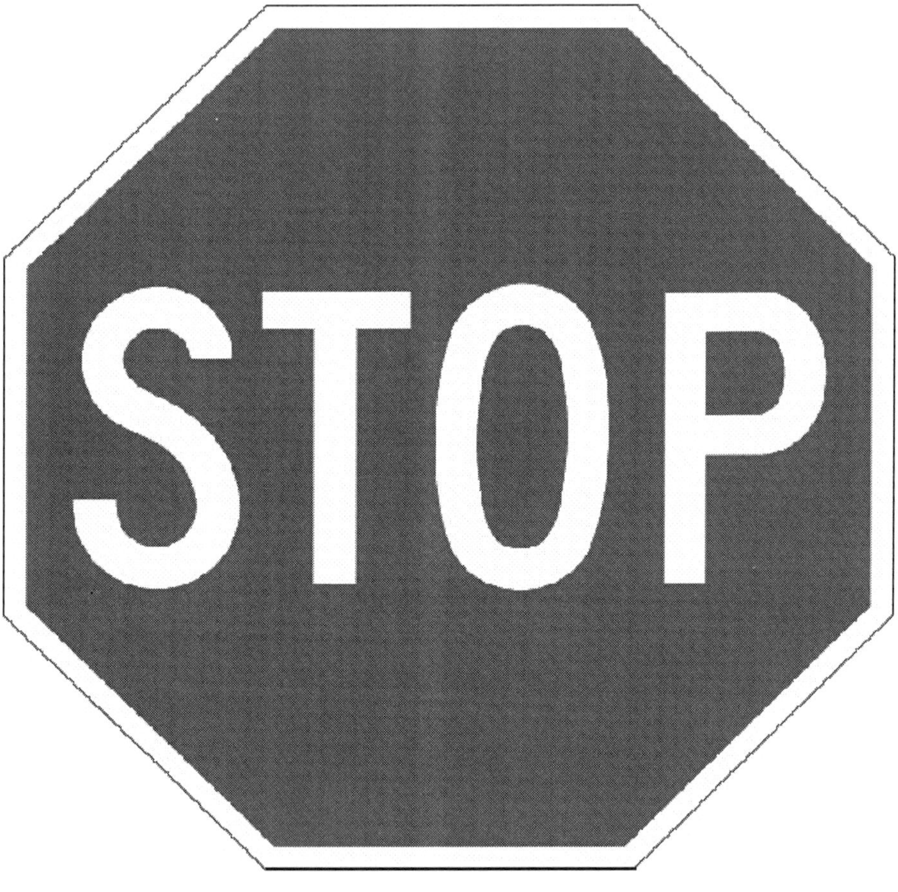
STOP

CAUTION

THIS BOOK IS not for quitters!!! If you do not possess the desire to achieve, look no further. But if you are striving to be the best, YES this is the book for you.

RECOMMENDATIONS

THIS IS AN excellent resource book for those just starting out in the pursuit of success & their personal goals, and also for those who have already achieved success. This must have book is a reminder of what it takes to succeed, because we often need to be reminded to stay on top and to be competitive.

-James Mitchell, Ret. Councilman Warrensville Heights OH, Business Leader, Entrepreneur

I give this book an "E" as in Excellent! It is in my sincere opinion that your readers will benefit tremendously from your perseverance and effort towards this book. You will make a profound difference in the lives of young people everywhere.

-Brendolyn G. Brister, Administrator, Educator (K-8) Cleveland, OH

ABOUT THE AUTHOR

BYRON JACKSON IS currently a doctoral student intern, and will be a Doctor of Chiropractic within the next 8 months. He is a multi-gifted motivational speaker, author, business consultant, fitness consultant, and health advisor. He is founder and president of THINK LARGE INTERNATIONAL, which seeks to help young people, and adults alike to achieve their goals and purpose in life . . . He is dedicated to inspiring people to develop an enthusiastic attitude for success and believing God's promises for their life.

From middle school to college Byron Jackson has participated in many school activities, held leadership positions, and has received recognition for high achievements. He has won other awards for his involvement in oratorical contests and has received special recognition from the board of education, local clergymen, and elected officials. In 2001 & 2002 Byron Jackson became a 2 time NCAA Football National Champion with Mount Union College, and in 2005 became a member of the PHA – AF&AM.

PREFACE

"GOD IS NO respecter of person." Success and failure are forks in the road that are chosen by your level of expectation. The misconception that success is reserved for the upper class is only a myth. In reality we were all born to be champions, but it takes dedication, hard work, persistence, singleness of purpose, and the nerves of steel to achieve your goals.

INTRODUCTION

FROM THE WORLD'S view the words "3, 2, 1, blast-off!" Represent the descent of astronauts embarking on yet another discovery of our mysterious universe. However, if prior to takeoff, the engines aren't fueled, primed and ready to go; blast-off would mean nothing.

In life the mind like an engine must be set, checked, and ready for success. Success, like an astronauts' take-off must be planned and prepared for.

This book does not in any way support self-pity or lack thereof. It seeks to identify and draw out the greatness housed in us all. *Stand Tall, Dream Big, Think Large, I Dare You!* Is the manual for programming yourself, your children, family, and employees for success. If you are one of the many, who intend on elevating your mind, spirit, and soul, then this is a must have for your life. Success is not determined by your past experiences. You must raise your level of expectations and toughen your skin, like an alligator with out the bumps to journey the road of success. The keys to success that were used in ancient times are the same keys used today. Those success keys are so simply laid out in this easy to read book, that there is no doubt, you will be able to unlock the treasures of wealth, prosperity, and wholeness.

CHAPTER 1

GOALS

> "Without setting goals, life is nothing but a whirlwind passing you by."
>
> Byron G. Jackson

GOALS ARE SIMPLY assignments and responsibilities one has set for themselves, and has made a vow to complete them at, all cost. In 2006 Peyton Manning quarterback of the Indianapolis Colts threw 4 touchdown passes against the Cincinnati Bengals who only allowed their previous 5 opponents a combined score of 35 points. After the game a reporter asked Manning: "*Do you feel weird winning?*" He replied, "*No, I feel weird losing.*" Once you conceive a goal-orientated mentality, you'll expect nothing but the best for your life. Goal after goal will continue to be met in your life, and you yourself will feel weird if you don't accomplish your goals; because goal setting is the first step toward becoming a winner.

Before any great accomplishment or feat is obtained, a goal must first be set in place. Every morning you awake, your goal should direct your day-to-day activities. If you don't set forth a goal, you will be no more than an arthropod wondering about the wilderness with no basis; designating your life without purpose. The reason why most individuals don't become successful and accomplish their goals is not because they set forth intangible goals. It's because they don't separate their short term and long-term goals. Everyone wants to strike it rich and have exuberant success; however that's not enough to qualify and maintain a goal. Long-term goals are the end results an individual wants to achieve. It could be to make the Deans list, purchase a home, start a new business, or become senior partner of an executive firm, or run for political office. There is no limit to what a long term goal could be; it only depends on how big an individual wants to dream. One day someone dreamed of becoming President, and they did. Your long-term goals are only a reflection of your level of expectation. Some people want to soar high, and some want to soar very high amongst the eagles in the sky. There are some individuals who have long term goals of becoming the leaders of tomorrow, and one day they will. In order to consciously become aware of something you must consistently see it and hear it. It's no different for achieving long term goals for your life. You must write them down, tape them to the wall, and read them before you start your day and before you go to sleep. Your sub-conscious will then confirm your victory spiritually even before your goals have been accomplished, and success after success will begin to manifest in your life.

I once wanted to grasp a great success over night, and my father recited this popular saying to me: "How do you eat an elephant; one bite at a time." I then knew I had to prioritize my goals. I still had my long-term goal in tact, but I had to incorporate my short-term goals first.

Short term goals are progressive steps that when accomplished, lead to the manifestation of your long-term goals. Short-term goals are regularly ignored, because of the misconception that dreams are acquired over night. Everyone knows the legend that at the end of the rainbow, is a pot of gold. However, only a few are willing to take on the journey of traveling the distance. The accomplishments of short-term goals are valuable to the advancement of life. Next to your long term goals, should be a list of 5 to 10 ways you can improve and accomplish your goal, therefore, being defined as your short-term goals. Take the manager of a prizefighter for example: His long-term goal is to make his fighter a world champion, whether he's a lightweight, middleweight, or heavyweight fighter. But the manager knows that the championship fight isn't going to come over night. While never losing sight of his long-term goal, he incorporates the short-term goals daily, setting the time and days for training and sparring. Gradually his fighter gets bigger, faster, and stronger, and the manager knows his fighter is ready for a bout. The first fight the manager arranges is as vital as is the exchange of oxygen and bodily fluids are in regulating the body. This first fight is not against the champion of the world; it's against another boxer that matches well against the skills and talents of his fighter. Once the manager's fighter wins one fight, he continues to arrange matches for him that he is highly favored to win. This builds his confidence and faith, while approaching the long-term goal one step at a time. As match after match is won, so are the short-term goals, one at a time. Years later after sweat, blood, and tears have been exhausted and their short-term goals have been met, the bell sounds and a world champion is crowned king of the world.

There are going to be times when you won't meet your short-term goals, but don't cave in, give up, fold, and quit. When Ethel Kennedy had to deal with the death and, the assassination of President John Kennedy, and his brother Attorney General Robert Kennedy, everyone expected her to come tumbling down. But she didn't tremble and collapse, her response to her critics was: "*If a bird can sing after a storm, so can I.*" Don't accept self-pity for your life, no matter what happens. If you fall to you knees before you accomplish your goals, dust yourself off and start again. Every successful individual has experienced misfortunate circumstances. But their claim to fame is that they kept on trying when many others quit. The same applies for achieving your goals, always stay committed to them, see them, read them, and envision them taking place now. Never become deterred or derailed from your course, because there is a crown waiting for you. Remember, we can all be champions.

> "If life was easy, being a success would mean nothing. Success is not for fair weather agents, you must have nerves of steel and a cast iron stomach to be successful."
>
> Byron Jackson

Napoleon Bonaparte didn't become "one of the greatest commanders ever to have lived" in the blink of an eye. He calculated every move he and his army made, and there were times they fell short of their goals and deadlines. Hardship and struggles did present themselves but he did not allow it to stop him nor his army; they kept moving forward and as its written Napoleon and his army surmounted, "acquiring control of most of continental Europe."

When you get close to your goal, and adversities approach, know that you were born for it. You are about to step into your dreams and be an influence to those around you and to generations to come. Don't allow the feelings of negativity, fear, and adversity infect you and your goals. With continuous effort and focus you will succeed.

> "Tough people, always outlast, tough times."
>
> M. G. Jackson

Your goals aren't going to manifest overnight. Just like a gardener knows their garden isn't going to sprout forth in a days' span. You must possess the stamina of a marathoner, pushing forward without the option of stopping and giving up.

The enemy (the devil) is real and his job is to prevent you from achieving your goals through suggestion; but God is all-powerful and you can "do all things through Christ who strengthens you," Holy Bible. When you get close to your goals, the devil will try to deter you from your victory. It's natural to be scared during a fire, a car accident, or any life-threatening event. But when you're on your way to going to another level, don't fear. For it is written that God has not given us the spirit of fear, but of power, love, and a sound mind. For it's been said: "Fear of failure, stops everyone but the champions." The enemy is going to say to you "you are going to make a fool of yourself, you're not qualified to achieve these goals," but don't let that fear grip you. Any negative thing that you have experienced will attempt to consume you and take you over. But you must dig deep down, mustard up all the confidence and strength you have to kick down the door of fear because once you've made it to the other side, you'll realize that the panicky sweat and butterflies were nothing. When you're closing in on your goal don't associate, affiliate, or entertain negative people who will doubt you. Every individual on the planet gives off a source of energy; it can either be positive or negative. If you become associated with someone possessing a negative pessimistic attitude, you will feel lousy, down, and defeated. Scientist and researches have proven the phenomenon that oil and water don't mix. Likewise, positive people don't mix with negative people, because they know if that negative attitude catches hold to them it'll be like a wildfire spreading uncontrollably throughout their psyche. And they'll become a gruesome, negative being, instead of living life in overflowing fullness.

Don't defeat yourself because of the negative energy you have tapped into. Any successful organization or business whether it is positive or negative, channels the same energy from one person to another. The reason why the McDonalds Corporation can open a successful franchise on any street corner in any country is because each person involved channels their energies from one another towards a common goal. Bishop Eric K. Clark of Ohio said this best when he said, "Your connection, affects your direction." Surround yourself with individuals who are interested in success, and watch your goals propel.

An English professor once told a student that he'd never become a writer, because that was his weak area. However, that student didn't feed on that negative energy, instead he believed in himself. That student is the renowned Dr. Robert H. Schuller, best selling author time and time again.

CHAPTER 2

CONFIDENCE

> "Lack of confidence discourages superiority, which results in mediocrity that sets the path for inferiority."
>
> Byron Jackson

WILLIAM PENN PATRICK said: "Courage is the one ingredient that separates the weak from the strong, the successful from the weak, and the great from the average." Always stand firm in your beliefs. No matter if you come short of the finish line, keep trying, and see yourself tackling your goals and the tasks at hand. You have the favor of God upon your life, and you should expect nothing but the best for yourself. Allow nothing or no one to tell you otherwise. Envision your goals as being above the norm. Your standards must be top of the line. In order to be a king, you must act like one. It's not enough to just speak words, just to hear yourself say them, you must live what you say, believe it, and make it happen. With a strong level of confidence your achievements are right there for the taking. Don't just be a dreamer do something to bring your goals to life. Nurture your goals with confidence as you would a seed with water and sunlight. Understand confidence is your driving force to greatness. Believe you are a competent individual, skillful in creative thinking, and you will have the ability to succeed and solve any problem that presents itself. Capacity is a state of mind, if you believe in God and yourself more, you can do more. Records are meant to be broken, a well can always be dug deeper, buildings can be built taller; so don't settle into a comfort zone because you can never meet your full potential. Pastor Willie M. Pope once said: *"Don't think small; think big, because I'm going to think large."*

Believe in yourself with all your strength, believe you can and you will succeed. God wishes above all that you prosper and be in health. He promises that you can do all things through Christ Jesus who strengthens you. Believe God's word, believe it applies to you, and keep pushing on. Keep going; keep moving forward and sooner or later the world will make way for you. Confidence is the stepping-stone to success.

Muhammad Ali believed he was the greatest of his profession. And because of his belief in himself the world did make way for him. As history denotes, Ali is one of the greatest fighters of all times. Confidence discriminates against no one; if you think you can, you can. If you think you can't you can't. Always remember the 10 most powerful words in the English language are "*If it is to be, it is up to me.*"

How you perceive yourself is how others will perceive you. Don't ever tell yourself you feel broke, busted, or disgusted; instead have a king's mentality, and your destination of prosperity will be on express delivery to you. If you let a weak poverty stricken attitude reign over your life you'll resemble that of weakness. It doesn't matter what happened in your past, with supreme confidence, you are heir to the thrown of success. Feel good about yourself, and don't let the views of other people affect you; because while they're talking about you, you'll be eating at the king's table.

> "If you have no confidence in self, you are twice defeated in the race of life. With confidence, you have won even before you have started."
>
> Marcus Garvey

Don't let anyone steal your confidence. Individuals are going to talk about you, ridicule you, and maybe make false claims about you; but steadfast because your victory is right around the corner. The fact that someone is taking the time out to acknowledge you means you made that much of an impact on their life. And when it's all said and done, sooner than later, you'll be the CEO of your success. Your life's purpose will be so full; those same individuals will be asking you for a job.

Marking your life as a success is uncomfortable. It's going to require stepping out of your comfort zone. Sacrifices must be made, pain is going to attempt to conquer and torment you. But that's only a test of your confidence level. Success is not going to drop from heaven into your lap; you must prove yourself worthy. Cut that infection of self-doubt away from you, before it destroys you. The difference between a person with mental toughness and those who lack it is not strength and brawn. It's the might, determination, and desire that are possessed in the heart.

You are already equipped with the tools needed to achieve, in every area of your life. You must dig down deep and pull it out; no one is going to do it for you. Diamonds, one of the most precious jewels of the earth wasn't discovered because of wishing and hoping, it took someone with guts to search them out, and dig them up. The only thing guaranteed in this world is that hard times and pain are going to confront you. Be thankful because those same hard times and pains give you the opportunity to strengthen your confidence and build your character to overcome the adversities of your life. Your spirit of confidence must be bigger than Godzilla. To be a champion, you've got to know you're great, you're the best, you're the beauty of life, and able to accomplish anything. When you possess supreme confidence in yourself, someone should be able to hand cuff you, blind fold you, and drop you off in some undisclosed location in Timbuktu and you should still come up a winner.

CHAPTER 3

ATTITUDE

> "Walk tall, think positive, make a difference, dream big, I dare you!"
>
> Wanda Jackson

T HE MIND IS a vital aspect to the body and soul. A persons mind is the bridge to riches, fame, success, and even eternity. And as the old saying goes: "a mind is a terrible thing to waste." Throughout history, it has been proven that you are what you think. And it does not matter if you are from the lowest class of poverty or the royalist of families. Don King, the promoting giant said it best when he said "Only in America, can a person be born with nothing and hob knob with kings and queens." He discovered the secret that many spend a lifetime searching for. That is your present situation and circumstances mean nothing if you stay focused on your goals. Your vision and determination will determine your destination. There will be many who make the claim, "but you don't understand my situation" or "God let it happen for a reason." And as a human being the easiest thing to do, is to make excuses and blame others for our present situation. Until you accept responsibility for your own life and ventures, you will never be able to reach the maximum potential of your goals.

The truth of the matter is, God is not a puppet master and does not wish to control our everyday actions. God has granted each person in the world free will, that's why where you spend eternity, is solely up to you. Along with free will, God has empowered us with supreme favor, but it is no one to blame but ourselves if our supreme favor does not resonate because of our unwillingness to take action and act on our goals.

There are many illustrations of ordinary people whose goals propelled them to surreal success; from Edwin C. Barnes, Reginald F. Lewis, to the influential men & women of the 21ST century. The art of goal setting and decisive thinking was immensely displayed by one of our nations most esteemed leaders, President Abraham Lincoln.

Through historians it is known that Abraham Lincoln was elected President of The United States of America in the year eighteen hundred sixty. Nonetheless, few know of the many adverse conditions President Lincoln had to subdue and overcome through decisive thinking. For twenty-seven years President Lincoln was presented with discouragement in almost every venture he pursued. From being unsuccessful in business, being defeated in over a half dozen political positions, and having a nervous breakdown. If many were to place themselves in the shoes of President Lincoln during this time, they would have given up on the very existence of life after the first or second misfortune. Not including the threatening health conditions, or ridicule they would have been subjected too.

Over a century ago, President Lincoln mastered the art of goal setting and decisive thinking, which still holds true today.

He refused to accept defeat, failure, or expect misfortunes. President Lincoln did not think of himself as a failure or in a class of inferiority, but had a goal of being a success. He believed firmly that he deserved all of the accolades of a successful leader. In return he achieved superior results and held the most prestigious office of all: President of The United States of America. You must grasp a strong hold to the principles of Dr. Frederick K. C. Price, which are to: "Cultivate your mind that you will be a success (a winner); no matter if no one else on the planet will, you will succeed."

Make no mistake about it, there will be road bumps, but if you always take another step forward, you will be closer to your victory. It does not matter how many times a man gets knocked down in a bout that determines the winner, it is the champion that remains standing and waving his arm high, who is remembered in the end.

FAILURE:

I've missed more than 9,000 shots in my career. I've lost almost 300 games. 26 Times I've been trusted to take the game winning shot and missed. I've failed over and over again in my life. And that is why I succeed.

Michael Jordan

Through the teachings of Dr. Creflo A. Dollar the influence of thinking has been further examined: It was said, "Before the growing of a fruit, the roots must first be established." One must first firmly believe a change will occur, before the rewards of abundant life and prosperity are harvested. Dr. Dollar explains that, in order to feel different, you must think different:

WORDS → THINKING → EMOTIONS → DECISIONS → ACTIONS → HABITS → CHARACTER → DESTINATION

The words you see, hear, and say effect your thinking; your thinking then drives your emotions, your emotions alter the decisions you make, your decisions determines your actions, your actions decide your habits, your habits define your character, and your character constitutes your destination.

You can apply this principle to every aspect of your life; your job/profession, relationships, social life, etc. If you continuously harbor negative, indecisive, self-pitiful thoughts the outcome of your destination will be a devastating loss to you.

SELF-PITY

I never saw a wild thing feel sorry for itself.
A small bird will drop frozen from a bough
without ever having felt sorry for itself.

D. H. Lawrence

What ever your situation is, it can be changed. If it is a professional move you are self-conscious about, tell yourself "you can, and you will achieve it." You must know you are capable of mastering whatever craft you are pursing and you will. "As long as the earth endures, seedtime and harvest . . . will never cease."-Genesis 8:22, The Holy Bible

Dr. Dollar expounded Genesis 8:22 by using the analogy of that of a farmer: "To a farmer a bag of seeds is priceless, however if those seeds are kept in storage and never used they are worthless." But when a farmer plants seeds, he knows his intended harvest must go through a maturation process. The farmer knows the maturation process is going to take some duration of time, and one day his intended harvest will blossom and flourish despite the rain sleet or snow that may come along. Your seed is keeping the right attitude and decisive thinking. Do not encapsulate self-pity, keep a positive attitude, stay focused on your goal, and sooner or later your goals and aspirations will blossom like a fresh rose. If you plant your seed of a positive attitude and decisive thinking your harvest will produce a persona and zeal that is so radiant; all of the joys of life will be drawn to you.

How is it, that at a time when the entire nation was at a period of economic stagnation Thomas J. Watson Sr. seemed to be "depression proof?" Thomas J. Watson Sr. established International Business Machines CO. (IBM) on one word "THINK." At the entrance of the IBM salesman school the top step and front door housed the words "THINK" on them. Watson Sr. kept a certain attitude, and demanded nothing less from his salesmen. A billion dollar corporation built its foundation not on the wish factor, but on a positive attitude and decisive thinking. This is your moment to uplift your wellbeing, through a determined heart and with every cell in your body. It is imperative that you tell yourself daily: *I will succeed, I will never give up, I am not a second-class citizen, and I am a success because God has favor upon me.* Believe this with all your heart.

CHAPTER 4

TAKE ACTION

> "Life is like a vapor, it's here for one moment then gone forever. Go for it, you only live once, so go at it, do something big, do something large in your life!!!"
>
> Byron Jackson

SOME PEOPLE IN life do nothing to achieve their goals, then they blame everyone else: that they got a bad break, they were at the wrong place at the wrong time, it wasn't meant for them to have this or that, life is unfair, they were born on the wrong side of the track, they're waiting to hit the lottery, or waiting for their ship to come in, they missed the horse by a hair, their rich relative played favorites and they were left out of the inheritance, or someone swindled them. You've heard all the reasons and many more excuses why they didn't make it or achieve their dream. The fact of the matter is, you have to take action; you have to put your plan into action. You have to pursue your goal; you may have to start small at first, but start, no matter how little your steps. You have to do something positive in the direction of your goal or dream. If you have thought up a good idea, or goal in your heart, but take no action toward your goal or idea nothing will happen. You have to put forth effort, a lot of effort; you have to take responsibility for your life, your dreams, your goals, your actions or your lack of action.

It doesn't matter if you have a great idea, a big goal, or great skills you must put them into action; an old Chinese proverb says: "A journey of a thousand miles starts with a single step."

> "Faith without works is dead."
>
> James 2:20, The Holy Bible

Every successful person has had down days, and extremely hard times. However, they've all got back up, brushed themselves off and started moving ahead again. Little by little the momentum picked up. Abraham Lincoln went from failure to failure many times before he became President of The United States of America. He experienced great losses, great adversities, but he was a man of action. He kept doing something positive in his pursuit of political office.

When adversities and hardship come to attack you, stand tall, dream big, think large. Know you've come too far to stop now. You may get knocked down, but never knocked out. If you sit around telling yourself you're sick, tired, or not qualified to achieve your goal you'll be miserable. When that happens get up, stir yourself up again, and get your dream back. Get fired up and go at it again, pursue your goal one more time. Dust yourself off, step up to the plate like a batter ready to swing, *take action*! Keep swinging, you might hit a home run or get on base, that'll put you in position to come home and score the winning run; but you have to keep trying, keep going forward!

Keep yourself stirred up! Today is a new day, a great day, and a gift from God. Tell yourself everyday "*Something great is going to happen to me today!!!*"

CHAPTER 5

Comfort Zone

DON'T QUIT

When things go wrong as they sometimes will, when the road you're trudging seems all uphill, when the funds are low and the debts are high, and you want to smile, but you have to sigh, when care is pressing you down a bit, rest if you must, but don't you quit.

    Life is queer with its twists and turns, as every one of us sometimes learns, and many a fellow turns about, when he might have won had he stuck it out. Don't give up though the pace seem slow, you might succeed with another blow.

    Often the goal is nearer than, it seems to a faint and faltering man, often the struggler has given up when he might have captured the victor's cup, and, he learned too late when the night came down, how close he was to the golden crown.

    Success is failure turned inside out, the silver tint of the clouds of doubt. And, you never can tell how close you are, it may be near when it seems afar, so stick to the fight when you're hardest hit, it's when things seems worst that you must not quit.

Unknown

There is an infinite amount of molecules available to this planet for the maturation and continuation of life. So why do some reach imaginable heights and then come tumbling down like a ton of bricks? It's because of their comfort zone. Truly successful individuals never stop innovating, and reaching higher. As long as breath is in you, never stop reaching for success. It's not good enough to be the best at what you do in your city, state, or even your country; be the greatest in the universe. Don't get comfortable because the sun is shinning in your life and the songbirds are chirping. You can never reach your maximum potential in life because there are always new avenues to be discovered.

It is the saddest thing in the world, to see wasted talent, or to hear someone tell the could've, should've, would've story. Don't give up on life, because life will never give up on you.

> "To get what you never had, you've got to do something you've never done!"
>
> Dr. Mike Murdock

BONUS CHAPTER FOR PARENTS AND GUARDIANS ONLY
Full Proof Success Formula

G IVE YOUR CHILDREN incentives to do well in school. Companies and organizations give incentives all the time to their employees and customers to meet sales quotas or use their products. They give away bonuses, trips, sports paraphernalia, or certificates. But some people never think about giving their children incentives or rewards for doing well in school: getting good grades, good test scores, and achieving in extra-curricular activities. Keep encouraging and motivating your children with words of positive affirmation. Always find something, no matter how large or small, to praise them for; then follow-up with a reward, accordingly. For example, giving your child $5.00 for every "A" and $3.00

for every "B" on their report cards in elementary school and middle school, and maybe $10.00 for every "A" and $5.00 for every "B" in high school; or maybe $100.00-$150.00 for merit roll and $175.00-$200.00 for honor roll or whatever you decide, but you get the picture. Giving rewards, incentives and words of encouragement, to achieve good grades . . . can inspire an entire generation to become not only athletic and entertainment stars, but business stars, doctor stars, attorney & judge stars, political stars, educating stars, etc.

I've seen this work in my own life and with people I know. When your child's academic status elevates, they'll then identify themselves as being just as smart as the next child. This carries from one grade to the next, building their confidence. The momentum picks up and there's no stopping them in accomplishing their goals and dreams in life!

Find out what motivates your child. Every child is different. But give them a reward or incentive and watch them go to work and their grades improve.

Important Fact: parents, grandparents, and guardians you must keep your end of the deal! You must give or do what you promise. Just like your job, if your boss told you and your co-workers, that if you make a certain quota or fulfilled a contract with a specific client, you will receive a reward or bonus. Now, how would you feel, if you and your co-workers met the quota, and your boss did not fulfill his promise? What would you think of him? Not good, that's for sure.

This formula works, TRUST ME!!!

> "There's only one way to succeed in anything, and that is to give it everything."
>
> Vince Lombardi

NOTES: _____

"Sometimes there is no next time, no second chance, no time out; sometimes . . . it's now or never."

Unknown

NOTES: _____

> "The best revenge is to have massive success."
>
> Paula White

NOTES: _____

ACCOMPLISHMENTS

-2007 Authored first book at the age of 24;
-2006 Passed proficient testing to become a Doctoral Student Intern, Life University College of Chiropractic;
-2005 New Member Certificate of Completion, World Changers Church Dr. Creflo A. Dollar, Pastor;
-2005 Participant of Life University Talent Show;
-2005 Official Member of PHA-AF&M;
-2004 Admitted into Life University Doctor Of Chiropractic Program;
-2003 Member of Mount Union College 2002 Division III NCAA Football National Championship Team;
-2002 Academic Wayne Manzilla Award Winner, Mount Union College;
-2001 Member of Mount Union College 2001 Division III NCAA Football National Championship Team;
-2001 Alpha Phi Alpha Fraternity Inc., Delta Alpha Lambda Chapter Scholarship Award Winner;
-2001 Co-Captain of Shaker Heights High School Football Team;

-2001   Carolyn Garvin Scholarship Award Winner, Shaker Schools Foundation;

-2001   Andrea Johnson Dare to Dream Scholarship Award Winner, Shaker Schools Foundation;

-2001   Western Reserve Society Oratorical Contest 3RD Place Award Winner;

-2001   Shaker Heights Public Library 3RD Place Dr. Martin Luther King, Jr. Essay Award Winner;

-2001   Antioch Baptist Church & Temple Emanu El, "Outstanding Students Who Exemplifies the Ideals And Visions of Dr. Martin L. King Jr." Award Winner;

-2000   Outstanding Perseverance Award Winner, Shaker Heights High School Football Program;

-2000   Minority Achievement Committee (MAC) Scholar co-leader, Shaker Heights High School;

-2000   Second year Varsity Award Letter, Shaker Heights High School Football Program;

-2000   Honor Roll & Merit Roll Student, Shaker Heights High School;

-2000   Spring Olympics 3RD Place Squat Lifting Award Winner, 2ND Place Flexibility Award Winner, 3$^{RD.}$ Place Hang-Cleans Lift Award Winner, 2$^{ND.}$ Place Dead-Lift Award Winner, Shaker Heights High School Football Program;

-2000   State of Ohio 2ND Place Dr. Martin L. King, Jr. Oratorical Contest Award Winner;

-2000   East View United Church of Christ Dr. Martin L. King, Jr. Cuyahoga County 1ST Place Essay Award Winner Dr. Valentino Lassiter, Pastor;

-2000   Guest Speaker of the "Dr. Martin L. King, Jr. Celebrate His Life and Legacy," sponsored by the Radical Ethnic Caucus;

-1999 Outstanding Academic Achievement Award, Shaker Heights High School;

-1999 Spring Olympics Squat Champ Award Winner, Shaker Heights High School Football Program;

-1999 Spring Olympics Dead Lift Champ Award Winner, Shaker Heights High School Football Program;

-1999 Two-Time Scholar Athlete Award Winner, Shaker Heights High School;

-1999 Iron Man of the Week Award Winner, Shaker Heights High School Football Program;

-1999 Spring Olympics 2ND Place Flexibility Award Winner, 3RD Place 20 Yard Dash Award Winner, 3RD Place Vertical Jump Award Winner, 3RD Place Long Jump Award Winner, Shaker Heights High School Football Program;

-1998 Omega Psi Phi Fraternity, Zeta Omega Chapter 3$^{RD.}$ Place Speech Competition Award Winner;

-1998 Junior Reserve Officers' Training Corps (J.R.O.T.C./Army) 1ST Place Speech Competition Award Winner, Shaw High School;

-1998 Awarded Rank of First Sergeant for Junior Reserve Officers' Training Corps (J.R.O.T.C./Army), Shaw High School;

-1997 Elected W.H. Kirk Middle School Student Government President;

-1997-1996 Member of W.H. Kirk Middle School Track & Field Team;

-1997-1995 Member of W.H. Kirk Middle School Football Team,

-1997-1995 Member of W.H. Kirk Middle School Wrestling Team;

Byron Jackson is always interested in receiving testimonials from his readers. To share your experiences from this book contact Think Large International.

To order copies of this book mail the form below along with check/money-order payable to: Byron Jackson, c/o Think Large International in the amount of $10.00 (per copy) + $3.00 shipping & handling.

A 15% discount will be assessed to orders of 100 copies or more.

THINK LARGE INTERNATIONAL
P.O. Box 201852
Shaker Heights, OH 44120
770-714-1157:PH

NAME:	_____
ADDRESS:	_____
	_____
	_____
PHONE:	_____
EMAIL:	_____
# OF COPIES ORDERED	
Total AMOUNT ENCLOSED	